A Human Menagerie

A Human Menagerie

Triumphs, Tragedies, and Cautionary Tales
in Verse

Written and Illustrated by Rob Kleinsteuber

outskirtspress
DENVER, COLORADO

The opinions expressed in this manuscript are solely the opinions of the author and do not represent the opinions or thoughts of the publisher. The author has represented and warranted full ownership and/or legal right to publish all the materials in this book.

A Human Menagerie
Triumphs, Tragedies, And Cautionary Tales In Verse
All Rights Reserved.
Copyright © 2013 Rob Kleinsteuber
v1.0

Cover and Interior Artwork provided by Rob Kleinsteuber All rights reserved - used with permission.

This book may not be reproduced, transmitted, or stored in whole or in part by any means, including graphic, electronic, or mechanical without the express written consent of the publisher except in the case of brief quotations embodied in critical articles and reviews.

Outskirts Press, Inc.
http://www.outskirtspress.com

Paperback ISBN: 978-1-4787-1434-7
Hardback ISBN: 978-1-4787-1412-5

Library of Congress Control Number: 2012923980

Outskirts Press and the "OP" logo are trademarks belonging to Outskirts Press, Inc.

PRINTED IN THE UNITED STATES OF AMERICA

for my mother,
who taught me to love truth

Acknowledgments

This book would not have happened without the help of others.

Special thanks are due to my partner, Bill Mould, who has given loving support throughout the 18 years that we have been together. His critical eye and complete honesty were evident when we were still courting, and I shared one of my lesser efforts written when I was a fervent young man. His response: "That's really awful." I knew right then he was a keeper. He has improved my poetry—and me!

My sister, Barbara Hamilton, has been privy to these poems since their creation and has always provided encouragement.

Outside of my family, the first person with whom I shared the poems in this book was my dear friend, Victoria Jackson, who has pushed me to publish for at least a decade. My close friend, Jack Adams, was catalytic to the creation of this book and has been instrumental throughout its evolution. Jack brings much good to the world. He introduced Bill and me to Poets House in New York City, where I was able to see some of Emily Dickinson's writings in her own hand.

I owe a debt of gratitude for the critical reading given the book by my friends, Jon Kula and George Rivers, whose fresh insights helped me polish the poems. I wish also to express my thanks to my friend, Francis Ying, whose complete professionalism in the studio and strong direction made recording the book a delightful experience.

Finally, I must express my appreciation to the many others who have helped me find my voice.

Contents

A Human Zoo	3
Arnold the Greeter	4
Old Miss Quigley	6
Betty Border	8
Martin Littleton, Empire Builder	9
Buster O'Bluster	12
A Smile Comes to Dolores del Sangre	15
Philo Crumrine and the Corporate Fathers	18
The Horrible Creatures	21
Mothball & Son. Fine Antiques	22
Miss Malinsky	27
A Covington Christmas	28
Mrs. Young	30
On the Eve of His Seventieth Birthday	32

Winifred Phyffe	36
Sergeant Quilty, Maker of Men	38
Dorothy Drudgewicke	40
Another Dinner/Sales Meeting with the Boss	42
The Boy on the Beach	45
Alas, Poor Torek	48
Hale Mary	51
Garrison Goodbody	57
Melody McMallidy	61
The Devil and Crazy Eddie	62
Ordelia O'Fonely	66
Rod Rockwell, Mountain Tamer	69
Closing Time	72
Dear Reader	74
A Sonnet on It	75

A Human Menagerie

Triumphs, Tragedies, and Cautionary Tales in Verse

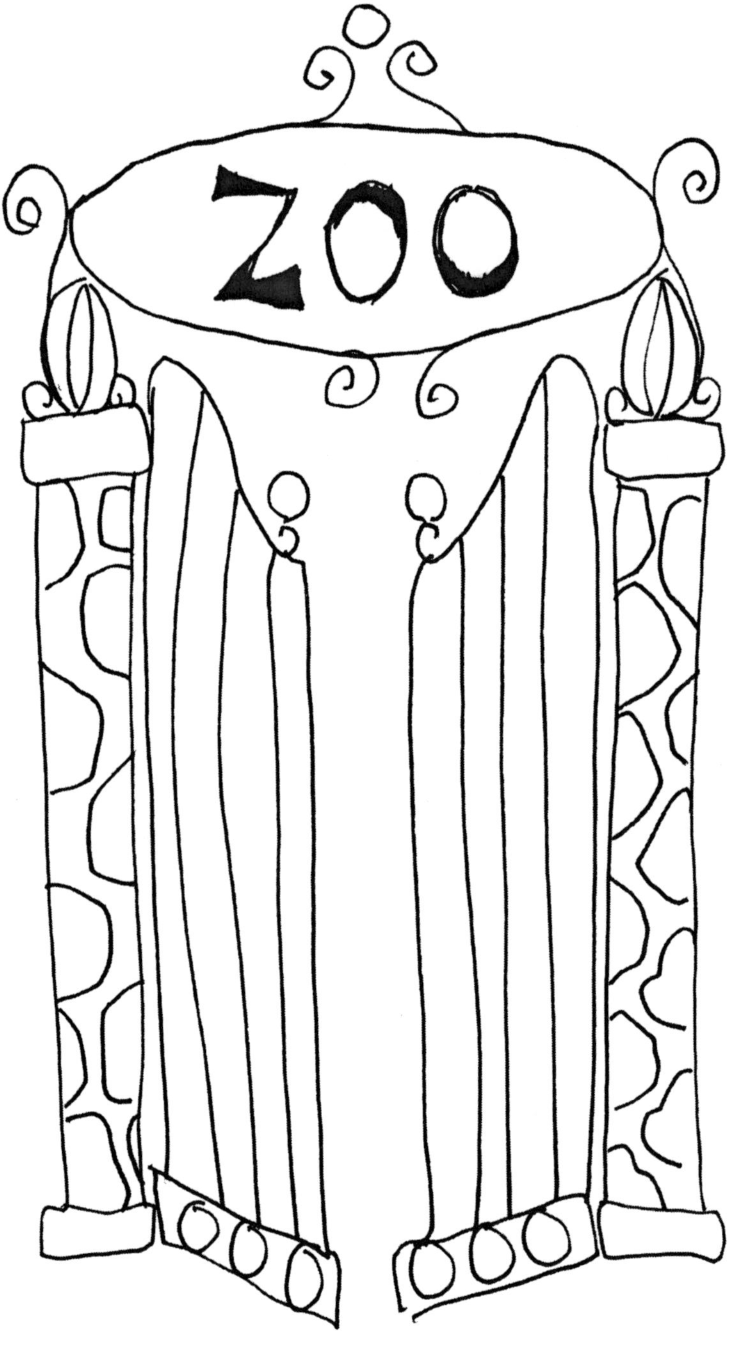
ZOO

A Human Zoo

When strolling through a human zoo,
You'll find some cages—very few—
That stand quite empty, side by side,
With locks unlocked and gates swung wide.

How can it be so few break free
When every cage contains a key?
The secret's this: the key that lies
Within each cage is of a size

Which only fits the lock that's for
The cage that's standing just next door.
And everyone who's caged can reach
Adjacent locks, so each by each,

All prisoners could free the next.
And yet, most of the caged, perplexed,
See just the world within the cage
They've forged themselves. So come, let's gauge
The souls that wait beyond this page.

Arnold the Greeter

The condo board, which wields control,
Decided to conduct a poll.
Result: No pets! No marmosets!
Not even goldfish in a bowl!

Although the rule was long in place,
The former chair just couldn't chase
Away the cat dear Arnold Sprat
Kept "secret" in his living space.

But then another resident
Was soon elected president.

This president was keen to rid
The building of all pets that hid
In secret lairs 'neath beds and chairs.
He'd rout them all! And so he did.

Old Arnold Sprat had nothing left.
With Baby gone, his heart was cleft.
His world destroyed, he faced the void.
And so he grieved—bereaved, bereft.

And now he finds he cannot bear
His flat without his Baby there.

A lobby chair's become his throne.
Both day and night the man is known
To nod, alas, to all who pass.
He's terrified he'll die alone.

And so with worry unremitting,
He still is sitting, still is sitting.

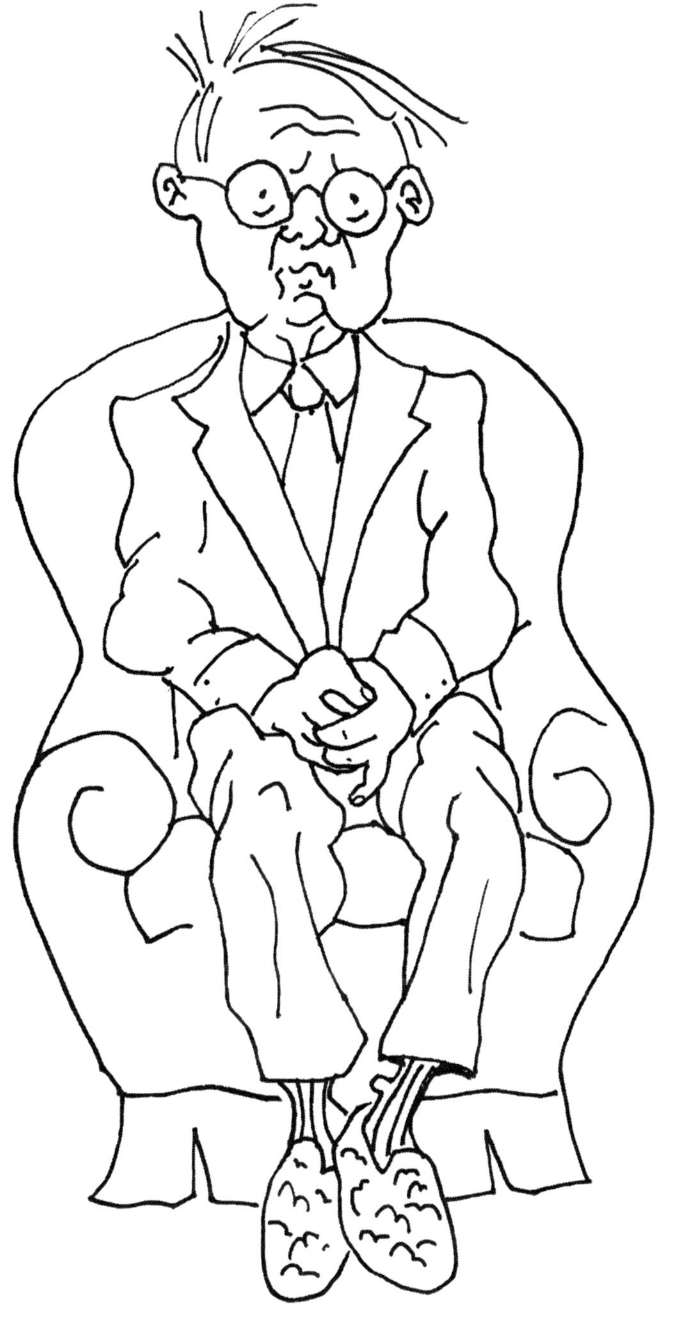

Old Miss Quigley

Miss Quigley loved cats. She had dozens and dozens.
Each cat that she owned had legions of cousins,
Brothers and sisters, score upon score:
They made a carpet on the floor.
And still Miss Quigley took in more!

Old Miss Quigley never wed,
Devoting her life to her cats instead.
To all of those who questioned why,
"They need me so," was her reply.

And when the authorities came to call,
There were cats in the parlor, cats in the hall,
Cats on each rafter, cats on each wall.
They said, "This will not do at all!
There are too many cats for a house this small!"

Miss Q just purred, "Please follow me.
I've one more cat you'll want to see."
But halfway down the cellar stairs,
Miss Quigley sneezed. "These cold, damp airs!
I'll just go up and get my shawl.
But go on down, and please don't fall."

She'd barely shut the basement door
When from below, a mighty roar!
"So glad they came," she sighed, "for Hector
So enjoyed his last inspector."

She thought of the day she found the new stray—
A rather large kitten who wandered her way.
And not till he grew did it dawn on Miss Q
The cub was a lion escaped from the zoo!

Old Miss Quigley finished her tea
And went to the basement door.
"Come, Hector, dear. It's time for our nap.
But try not to burp or snore."

We leave Miss Quigley, kind and sweet,
Asleep with Hector at her feet.
And hanging above them the sampler she made:
Our every kindness is repaid.

Betty Border

Betty Border was a hoarder,
But she couldn't stand disorder.
Logged each item she acquired
In a notebook, spiral-wired.
Kept the notebook in a binder
By the door so they could find her
If it all collapsed around her.
It collapsed. They never found her.

Martin Littleton, Empire Builder

He begins in mid-October
When the weather, turning sober,
Makes one glad to be indoors,
Keeping busy, doing chores.

First come visits to the attic
Where the air is cold and static,
Then the delicate unwrapping
Of each friend who lay a-napping

All year long in tissued cartons,
Till awakened then by Martin's
Loving hand and warming breath,
Blowing off the dust of death.

Not so easy though to bid life
Come to all. His job of midwife
Calls for calipers and gauge,
Months of setting up the stage:

Skating lasses, sledding lads
Dressed in winter wools and plaids,
Ladies doing Christmas shopping,
Stores and homes with snowy topping.

Lighted windows, warm and cozy,
Painted cheeks all flushed and rosy;
Everything so quaint and cheery,
When it's done, it makes him teary

Just to gaze on his creation—
Not a village, but a nation
As it spreads from room to room,
Banishing all winter gloom.

Martin's walked a lonely course
In the years since his divorce:
Frozen meals, a Spartan diet,
Nights of reading, peace and quiet.

Doubtless Martin loved his Jessie.
Married life was just too messy:
Nylons hanging in the shower,
Little things that turned it sour.

He's fastidious and neat,
Five foot one in stocking feet,
Facial features finely placed,
Tiny hands and tiny waist.

Days are spent with row and column:
Spreadsheets—ordered, stately, solemn.
Fellow workers find him pleasant.
This year, as a Christmas present,

He's invited all to lunch:
Pizza, cookies, Christmas punch
(Juice and pop in equal measures),
Then a tour of all his treasures.

Martin's place is down the block,
Walking distance. He'll unlock
Thirteen Thirteen Newton Drive.
"Come on in when you arrive."

Heartbeat racing, breathing bated,
Martin's feeling agitated.
Punch can stain and cookies crumble.
What if someone takes a tumble?

Home to get the party ready,
Martin feels a bit unsteady.
There amid the urban sprawl
At his feet, he takes a fall.

Gasping, clutching, writhing, dying.
Dead. The guests soon find him lying,
Mouth agape and eyes unshut:
Gulliver in Lilliput.

Buster O'Bluster

Buster O'Bluster could kick up a duster.
He'd bellow and bully with all he could muster.
His wife bore his brunts. More than once he had thrust her
Downstairs, over chairs, and through doors as he cussed her,
Maiming and claiming he just couldn't trust her.
He'd grounds for suspicion: his lust was lackluster.

He was mean to her cats and the "brats" that he fathered,
But never once bothered to hug or to hold.
He was ugly and cold
To them—scolding, withholding
The love that they prayed for.
Crap like that wasn't what real men were made for.
"Babies and kids are what mothers are laid for."

He'd puff up his chest, self-impressed and important.
Was ever a despot so desperately potent?
He'd chomp his cigar like a star Mafioso,
Looking oh so intense—or at least, he'd suppose so.
The figure he cut as he'd swagger and strut,
His manly chin jutting! (Soon likewise his gut.)

His wife slipped out young. The Big C was her ticket.
And all of his kids in turn told him to stick it.
The decades have flown. My, how shriveled he's grown.
No wiser, but wizened. Alarmed and alone.
The hospital pillow is soaked with his tears.
They've taken his larynx but left him his fears.

What will last from the past that can comfort or show us
Any light in the night when it's Death come to throw us
To the void we've avoided till yawning below us?
What then to hold on to? To build on? To own?
Without form and substance, just love has been shown
To weather much better than iron and stone,
And last a bit longer than testosterone.

A Smile Comes to Dolores del Sangre

Dolores del Sangre is sullen and angry
Each time that we meet her. We hardly dare greet her.
She's always complaining. And when it's not raining,
She's ever so proud to point out the wee cloud
Alone in the distance, which, at her insistence,
Soon spreads like a stain.

Sure enough, it'll rain.

She rents a unit down the hall,
And makes it clear that we appall.
My partner, Bill, and I are gay.
And she is not. In any way.

She crosses herself every time that we meet her,
Her dark, circled eyes quite refuse to engage us—
Two bookworms unlikely to pillage or beat her.
Or does she believe that our "sin" is contagious?

She's surely known worse in her job as a nurse.

Her posture is stooped by the cross that she bears—
The woes of the world?
Or is it the weight of the cross that she wears?
Its surface is pearled
And it's tiny enough.
But the object is filled
With such burdensome stuff:

Transgressions, confessions, liturgical sessions;
Restrictions and fictions affirmed as convictions;
Rote memorization and self-abnegation;
The suffering Jesus
Whose baleful gaze sees us
Whenever we're sinning . . .
That's just the beginning.

But back to Dolores,
Who, standing before us,
Is closing the door to her dark little unit.
It reeks so of mothballs, we would just as soon it
Be closed or else hosed. Do the mothballs festoon it?

There was that episode, of course . . .
I shut our door with too much force—
Or so she claimed, and I objected.
Soon old complaints were resurrected.

Invective said and then forgotten,
At least by me, but sadly, not in
Her cerebral reliquary.
Nothing there is temporary.
Years flew by. I let things lie.
And then I had my coronary.

Waking from my operation,
I first discerned the nurse's station,
And then a figure walking to me,
Dolores-like, but not so gloomy.

Could that be she so filled with glee?
Were we in heaven? Had she forgiven
The time I hurled my wrath at her?
With mercy mild, she softly smiled.
"I'm here to change your catheter."

That's all she said as she leaned down
To move the sheet and raise my gown.
And in her hand she held a tube.
That's all she held. No love. No lube.

Philo Crumrine and the Corporate Fathers

Philo Crumrine's fiercely loyal
To the brass at Serpent Oil,
Calling them "the corporate fathers."
Humble Philo never bothers
Anyone with pleas for raises,
Never loafs and never lazes.
First one in and last one out.
Never is there any doubt
Crum will finish every task.
Weekend work as well? Just ask.

All the brass at Serpoco
See the profits running low.
Stock is down and they're in trouble.
Boom's gone bust and burst the bubble.
So there's only one solution:
Layoffs! Workforce diminution.

Philo Crumrine's rather blue.
He can't get an interview.
His experience is fine,
But the man is fifty-nine.
Still, he has his coming pension.
Oops! I somehow failed to mention
How the brass, in valiant measures
To protect their trove of treasures,
Perks, and salaries inflated,
Had all pensions terminated.
(Well, not theirs, but all the others.)
Corporate fathers can be mothers.

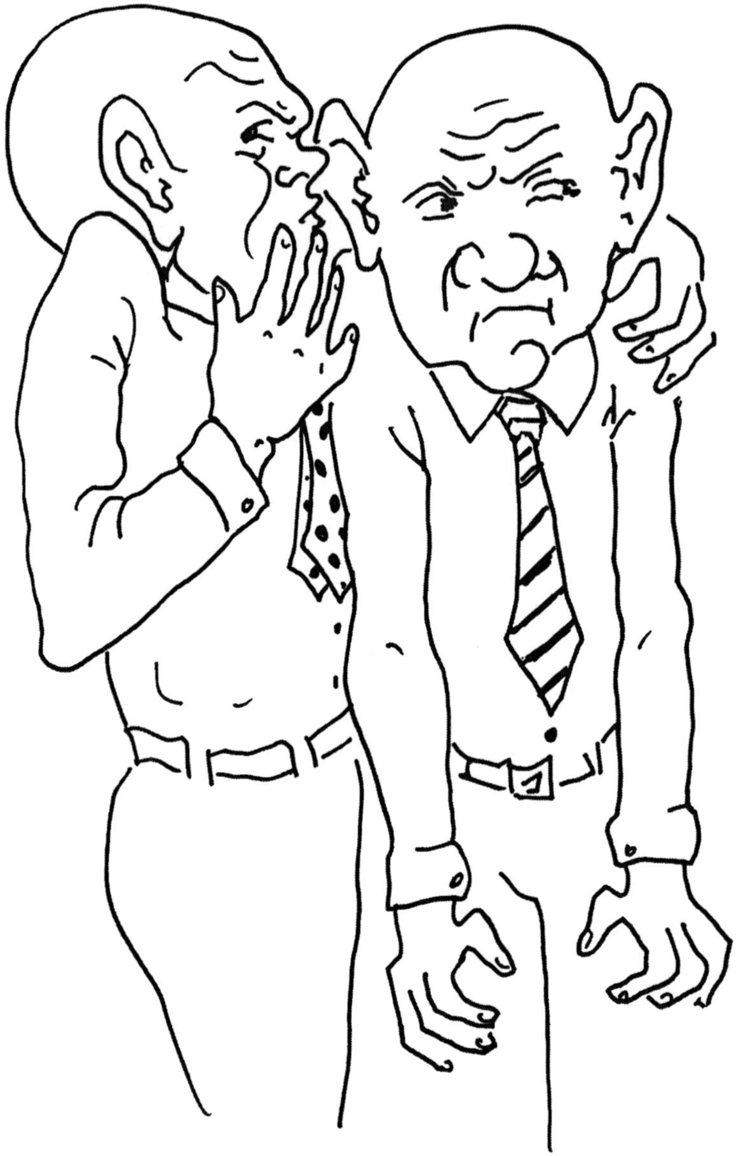

The Horrible Creatures

The horrible creatures are always lurking.
It doesn't matter where you're working,
The horrible creatures are resident.
It may be the company president,
Perhaps the executive secretary,
Or star on the rise. May eyes be wary:
The horrible creatures are very scary.

The horrible creatures get what they want.
For them the world is a restaurant.
If you're in the way of the big buffet,
You're plucked from the tray like a canapé.

The horrible creatures are always eager
To beat, berate, belittle, beleaguer.
And best when done from shadows, since
Such victims bear no fingerprints.

Get a new job or find a new state,
The horrible creatures are there. They wait.
The horrible creatures are out to get you,
But don't let a thing like that upset you.

The horrible creatures rule the planet.
It's been that way since God began it.
The fittest survive. It's only fitting.
At least, I guess, from where He's sitting.

Should germ or blow bring final gasp,
Or should I choose to clasp an asp
To self that I might slip their grasp,
Will I, right after my how-do-you-do,
Find God is a horrible creature too?

Mothball & Son. Fine Antiques

Behold Madame Mothball!
Isn't she enormous?
Judging from her scornful look,
I think she would reform us.

She doesn't care for children much.
She finds them energetic.
Their little voices, how they grate
And make her "palpitetic."

Although her voice is rather low,
She sneezes in soprano!
Dressed all in black, she looks so grand—
Just like a grand piano.

Her gown earns praise. Like Holland's dikes,
Its seams make one admire
Those fearless threads that brave the swell
And never seem to tire.

No matter what the subject is,
When Madame Mothball's speaking,
She always drops in Europe,
Where each year she goes antiquing.

She really needn't work so hard
To pass for "continental."
As it applies to size, she makes
Australia incidental.

Two clear, prismatic lozenges
Are swinging from her ears.
You know the kind. So elegant!
When hung from chandeliers.

The weight of them has stretched her lobes
Into a Chinese Buddha's.
Her small, black eyes swim back and forth
Like two penned barracudas.

Surveying any customers
Who seem the shifty sort,
She sits—a pillowed potentate,
A pasha holding court.

The shop is her seraglio,
Her son its guardian eunuch.
He smooths his bangs while polishing
A chest they found in Munich.
He's forty, still at home with Mom,
An antebellum monster—
Her home, I mean, whose walls since birth
Have lavishly ensconced her.

He holds her with a reverence
Most save for their religions.
He's very good. The perfect son.
His hobby's killing pigeons.

It breaks his heart, but kill he must
To save ancestral eaves
From droppings. So they drop instead
From poison that he leaves.

Exit Madame Mothball now.
It's home to take her nap.
She snaps and Sylvan drops his cloth
To help her with her wrap.

She rattles off a list of chores
To fill his afternoon.
For after work, another list.
Last order: "Get home soon!"

"I wish to sleep till eight tonight.
I'm feeling rather frail.
For dinner, fix me what you wish."
"Why not my famous quail?"

He smiles as she smacks her lips.
It's hours to prepare it,
For pigeon plucking's tedious;
And yet, he'll grin and bear it.

He really doesn't mind at all.
The meek, you know, inherit.

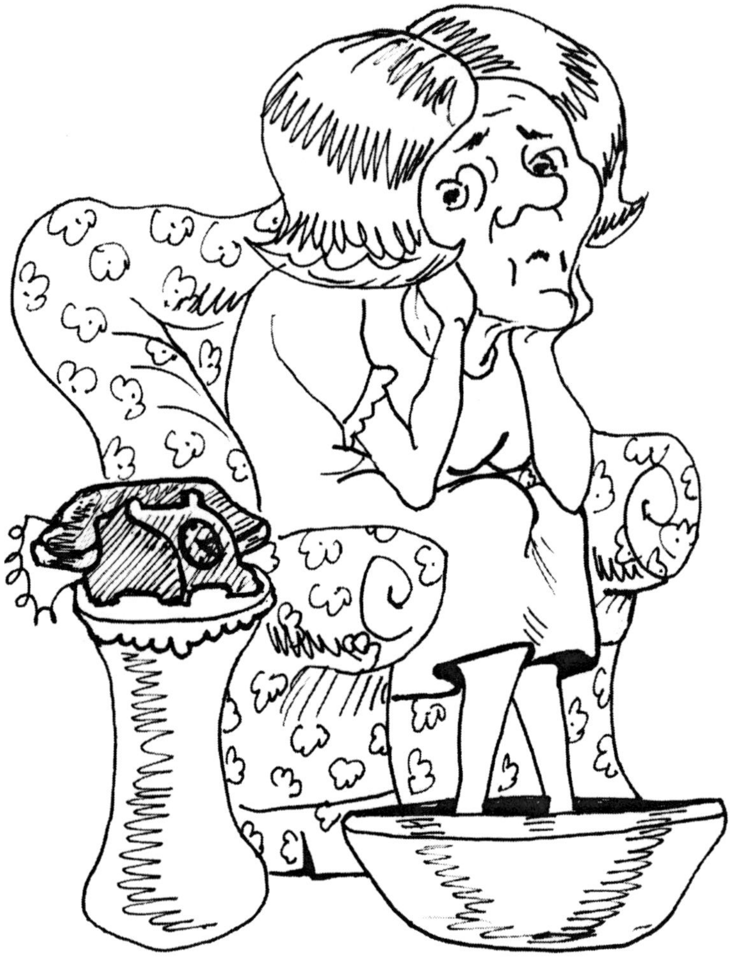

Miss Malinsky

Have you met Miss Malinsky, the local buttinsky?
She thinks she's the world's problem solver
Whom heaven has chosen for sticking her nose in
To business that doesn't involve her.

She keeps herself busy. It makes one quite dizzy
To watch the old girl at her labor.
A bee among flowers, she buzzes for hours
From neighbor to neighbor to neighbor.

She's ever so cheerful while getting an earful
Of gossip and scandal and rumor,
Which soon she'll be sharing. She thinks herself caring,
Since other folks' problems consume her.

Like two searchlights shining, her eyes, when she's dining
In restaurants, scan each darkened corner.
Should someone be spied with a "tart" at his side,
A call to his wife just to warn her.

When young ones are wed, she keeps track in her head
Of the days till their firstborn's debut.
If less than nine months, she calls neighbors at once
To announce her suspicions were true.

Her day's work complete, she sits soaking her feet;
Though nothing can take out the sting
Of sitting alone in the dark by the phone,
And hoping tonight it will ring.

A Covington Christmas

The Covingtons' Christmas is planned very early.
The presents are bought before shoppers turn surly.
And months before anyone worries of winter,
The holiday greetings arrive from the printer.
At bottom of each, like a government form,
"The Covingtons." My, but the typeface is warm.
A form letter—xeroxed—is stuffed into each.
It tells of promotions, the place at the beach,
Of Ashley at Vassar, of Hunter at Yale,

And Park's 40-footer, described keel to sail.
For closing, a "tail" of their prize Lhasa Apso.
A Westminster winner next year? Well, perhaps so.
Their holiday schedule, as full as a stocking,
Proceeds with a clockwork precision that's shocking.
Messiah and *Nutcracker*, function and fete,
The Covingtons come and they never come late.
The living-room tree is a sight to behold,
Bedecked all in heirlooms of crystal and gold.
Our Peggy's particular—does it herself.
When little, the children had longed to play elf
And help with the tree. So instead, as a token,
Their own in the basement. No heirlooms were broken.
Of course, they would stand at the threshold, both ridden
With yearnings to enter the sanctum forbidden,
Like natives who peer through the gates of resorts,
Or waifs at the windows of FAO Schwartz.
So clever that Peggy. The house is perfection,
With Christmas and Peggy in every direction.
Why, even the popcorn—she strings every kernel!
This bright lady's home was in *Ladies' Home Journal*.
It's now the big day. Peggy calls them to dinner.
(Did she say in the letter she's fifteen pounds thinner?)
Upstairs, in a whisper, Park says he must go.
The call's to his mistress—a Christmas hello.
And Ashley, ensconced in her bedroom of pink,
Prepares for the meal with a snort and a drink.
Park knocks at the bathroom, where Hunter's inside.
There isn't an answer, for Hunter has died.
But not without finally leaving his mark
On Peggy's impeccable Yule decor. Hark!
His blood decks the walls. It's a holiday scene.
The blood is so red and the bathroom so green.

Mrs. Young

I. The Clinic

Mrs. Young has had it lifted
Three times by a very gifted
Surgeon who has pulled and shifted
Sags and bags that always drifted
Right back into place within a space of seven months.

Once
She tried the lamb-cell shots.
Took lots and lots. Got youthful thoughts
And had the hot springs treatment by
A handsome Swiss who made her sigh.
Bliss. Transcendence! She adored it!
And her tip would well reward it.
(Why not? After all, she could certainly afford it.)

II. Back Home

That was seven months ago.
Her youthful glow's begun to flow,
As slush can never turn to snow,
No matter how you doctor it.
She's locked herself inside her room,
Flanked by makeup and perfume,
Assuming she can groom and sweeten
The proverbial dead horse that's usually beaten.

Mrs. Young, whose universe
Is Mrs. Young, would sooner verse
Herself in Self than join herself
To something greater than herself.

She sits there at her mirror, crying.
Her universe is old. And dying.

On the Eve of His Seventieth Birthday

Tonight the professor is dressing in leather.
He creeps up the staircase on tiptoe to gather
The toast and warm milk that he brought up to Mother
Ten minutes ago. Though she's not finished either,
Already the lady is out like a light.
Unusual rather. But fortunate quite.
The professor is dressing in leather tonight.

For sixty-odd years, he has crept up those stairs,
Blinked back his tears, joined Mum at her prayers;
With a book from the shelf, placed himself at her side,
And inwardly cried. And inwardly died.
And outwardly sighed.
For sixty odd years.
For tonight she had chosen her *Idylls of the King*.
Just the thing!
He would giggle if not for the sound.
The book and professor are both leather-bound!

On air the professor, now giddily gay,
Makes his way through the pall of the hall to his room
Where he'll bloom in the gloom like the moss in a tomb.
He opens the locks on a box 'neath his bed,
Then lays on the spread his self-presents, all dread-
Fully black. Black as death! Now he breathlessly thrills
To the valleys and hills that he smooths with his fingers.
His fantasy lingers on alleys that call him—
Attract and appall him!
Now nothing can stall him. He's breaking his tether!
Tonight the professor is dressing in leather.

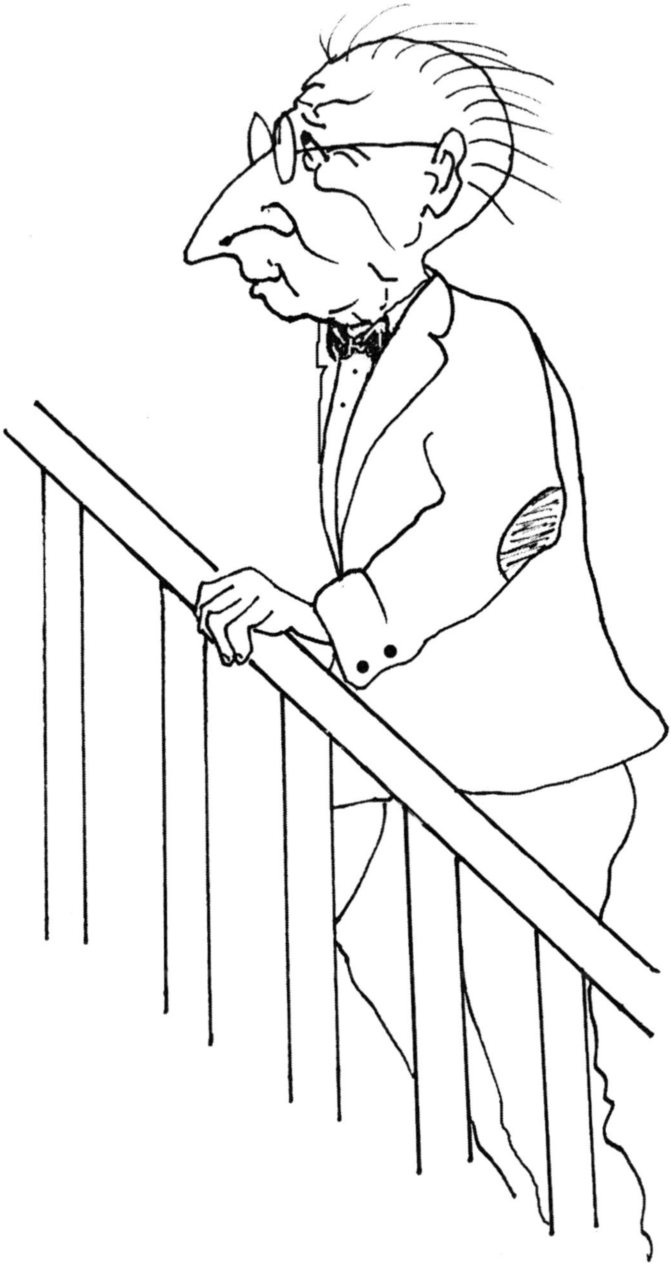

He's bound for a hot spot that's known as The Claw,
A smoky, forbidden place, livid and raw.
To enter its doors is like breaking a law!

And now the professor, completely upholstered,
Has bolstered his nerve to sufficient degrees
That at once he may seize this last chance at his freedom.
But if she should need him? Awake in the night
With a fright or a fever? He mustn't deceive her.
He'd better not leave her. He might have to save her!
What then? He must think.
The pills that he gave her (well, slipped in her drink),
They won't let it happen. She'll nap until morning.
And yet it's a warning. This feeling's a warning!

His studs in the mirror all sparkle like stars.
He paces in night like the beauty he seeks
In the alleys and bars and the leather boutiques.
He now thinks himself a ridiculous sight.
What beauty wants weathered, if leathered, physiques?
A pitiful fancy. "I'm still an old Nancy!"
Escapes from his lips as he slips off the pants he
Once viewed with such fevered delight.
Approaching his dresser, alas, the professor
Is wearing pajamas tonight.

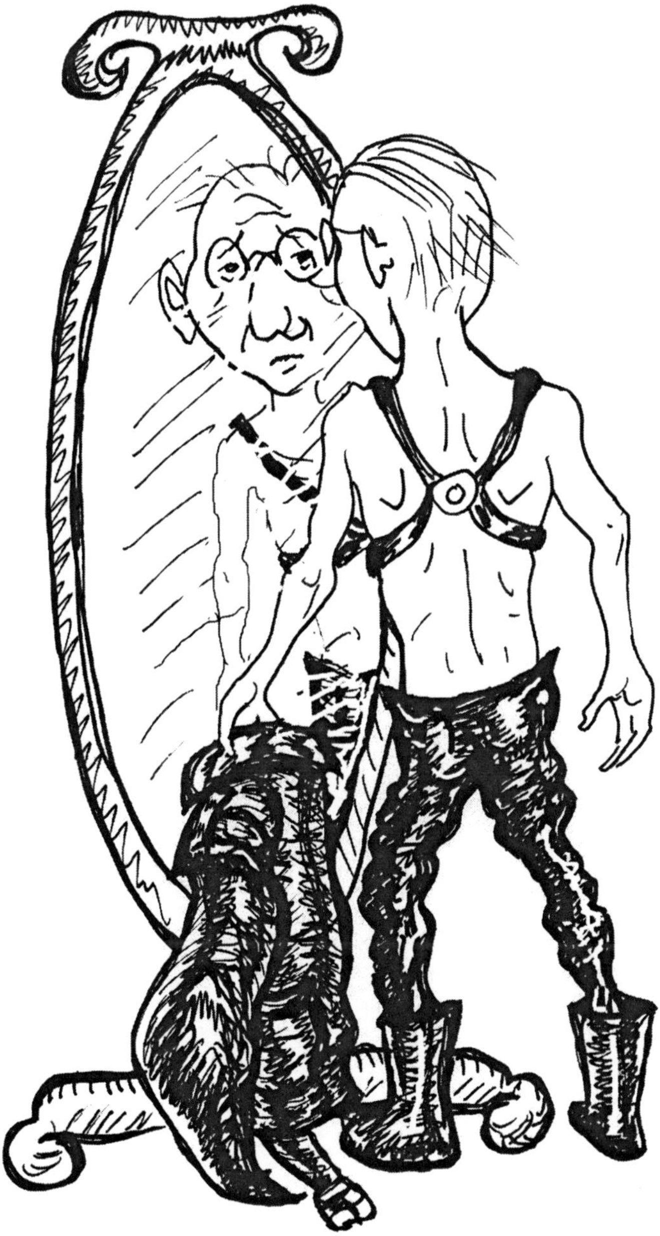

Winifred Phyffe

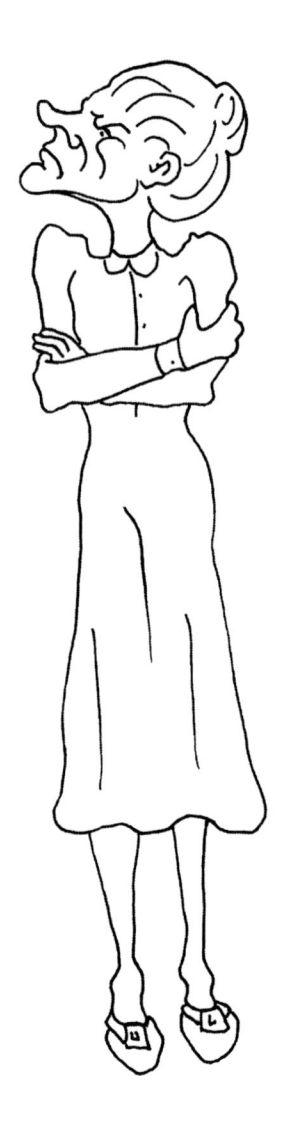

Winifred Phyffe, the minister's wife,
Has led a completely immaculate life.
Her virtue unflawed, she stands like a rod.
How else should one stand at the right hand of God?

Her judgment's as swift as His terrible sword.
She never shows mercy to those she has gored.
She'll leave that to Jesus. Old Yahweh's her Lord.

The minister's church is in Piney Woods Station.
She winces to think of its hick congregation.
He should have gone further. He could have done better.
She rues the black day that the minister met her.

Winifred Phyffe despises her spouse.
There's not one iota of love in their house.
Its silences deafen. Its chills send a shiver.
If this was the best that her husband could give her,
She'll give it right back! So she draws from her quiver
Each day a new arrow, attacks and withdraws—
Guerilla assaults on each one of his flaws.
Her arrows are tiny, but potent their tips:
They're coated with poison on leaving her lips.

Her war's lasted years, yet she's barely begun.
It's something to do with the death of a son—
The athlete, the scholar, her dear golden one.
The fault was her husband's. To this day she blames him.
The heat from her eyes always withers and shames him.

Winifred Phyffe's growing paler and thinning.
She doesn't yet know, but a tumor's beginning.
It grows like a fetus divinely implanted.
The keys to the kingdom are soon to be granted!
Let's hope there's a heaven for Winifred Phyffe,
Who's made such a hell for herself in this life.

Sergeant Quilty, Maker of Men

The sergeant drills at Camp Lejeune,
His pate as barren as the moon,
His body taut and tense and lean.
By God, this man is all Marine.

The sergeant boasts of slapping down
The smartass punks who play the clown,
And how he slams against the floor,
The sissy boys who plead, "No more!"

He shouts and curses loud and tough
And when each slacker's man enough
To stand up brave and strong and clean,
Then they, like him, are all Marine.

There was that time he pushed too hard.
The weakling died and he was barred
Until the judges said, "Not guilty.
Back to duty, Sergeant Quilty."

He struts among the iron weights
And lifts at least a dozen plates.
Part beast, part god, and part machine,
No doubt, this man is all Marine...

Until he smokes a cigarette.
And then there's something not quite "het"
About the way his fingers curl
Around the thing, and like a girl

He keeps his elbow at his waist.
Suspicions, though, are soon erased;
For any man who calls him "queer"
Is apt to lose a tooth or ear.

We leave him at the shopping mall.
It's crowded in his bathroom stall.
A boy of not yet seventeen
Is looking down on our Marine.

And just outside an undercover
Cop is seen to wait and hover.
Scandal! Will our Sergeant Quilty
Now be found to be not guilty?

Dorothy Drudgewicke

"Thanks, Dottie. You're wonderful." "Dottie, you're super!"
"Just give it to Dottie." "That Dottie's a trooper."

Meet Dorothy Drudgewicke. Near sixty. Not married.
Her job dedication is very unvaried.
She's quite the go-getter and such a self-starter,
So eager to please and so pleased to play martyr.

She's aching for love and taken for granted.
And no matter how much she's stammered or panted,
Acquiring daily a new tic or jerk,
They wind her up, praise her, and pour on the work.

She never says "no" to whatever they ask,
Yet mumbles and grumbles alone with the task,
While stealing occasional sips from her flask.

She needs to be needed. She wants to be cherished.
She longs to be longed for long after she's perished.
Her goal is quite simple: to be indispensable.
But nobody is. Come on, lady, be sensible.
Mohammed or Buddha or Christ on the cross,
The world never ceases whatever the loss,
But goes on quite nicely. And so will your boss.

She hits the ground running each day at full throttle,
And then hits the highway, and then hits the bottle.
And then hits a child one night on a bender—
A thud in the dark and blood on her fender.
And then hits the bottom. And then it's the end, or
Something close to it. "God, how could I do it?"
As custom requires, she quickly retires.
Then back to the bottle to help her get through it.

"Poor Dottie is calling again." "What's her worry?"
"I said I was busy. Her words sounded slurry."
"That's it! When she calls, we'll just be in a hurry."

Another Dinner/Sales Meeting with the Boss

Sic Semper Tyrannis!

Those of us who've had to sup with
Loud, obnoxious Larry Tupwith
Know he takes some putting up with.

He will soon regret his choices.
Eying other plates, he voices
Lust to sample yours or Joyce's.

Joyce, his fragile secretary,
Trembles meekly as his hairy
Wrist invades her lamb azeri.

Barking as he starts to chew,
He permits us all to view
How he turns her meat to goo.

Having mashed his spoils to pulp,
Barely having time to gulp,
Now he turns to Brian Culp.

Culp, our salesman in New York,
Thinks, as Tupwith raids his pork,
"Oh, to stab him with my fork!"

This time I won't mind a bit
When it's my turn to be "it."
See, I've added just a whit

Of some poison to my meat,
Gingerly and so discreet,
Saving what I dare not eat

For the boss. As is his habit,
There he goes. Now watch him grab it!
(I was wise to order rabbit.)

Tup will take some time to die.
If it's traced, my alibi?
Just that I could not deny

Boss man, mentor, lord, and idol,
Whose demands were hard to bridle.
He knew I was suicidal.

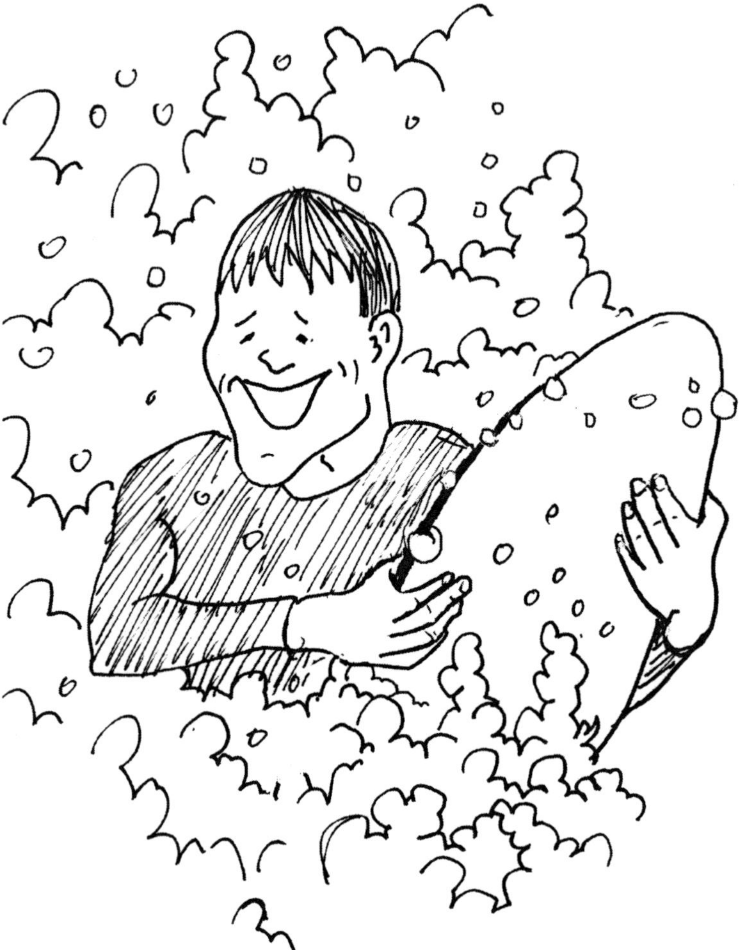

The Boy on the Beach

Gareth was golden,
Tanned and unflawed:
The image you hold in
Your head of a god.

A surfboard Apollo
Who crested the blue.
If Ocean should swallow,
He'd pop back in view,

So carefree and glad,
His laughter would reach
The boy's mom and dad
Who watched from the beach.

He aced all his courses,
His future assured
By many resources.
A siren then lured

The teen to the rocks.
She wouldn't let go.
No lectures or talks
Could free him from blow

Or crystal or speed.
The youth was now lost
To ruinous need.
No matter the cost,

His parents would pay
For expert or quack
In search of the day
Their boy would be back.

All therapy failed
And decades flew by,
He often was jailed,
But still they would try

With mortgages, liens,
And loans from the bank.
In time all their means
Of capital shrank.

His father still labors.
The debt they've acquired
Hangs on while their neighbors
Are snugly retired.

Awake with a start!
A telephone blast.
A blow to the heart.
It's over at last.

Nobody could save him,
Though both of them tried.
For all that they gave him,
He died. He still died.

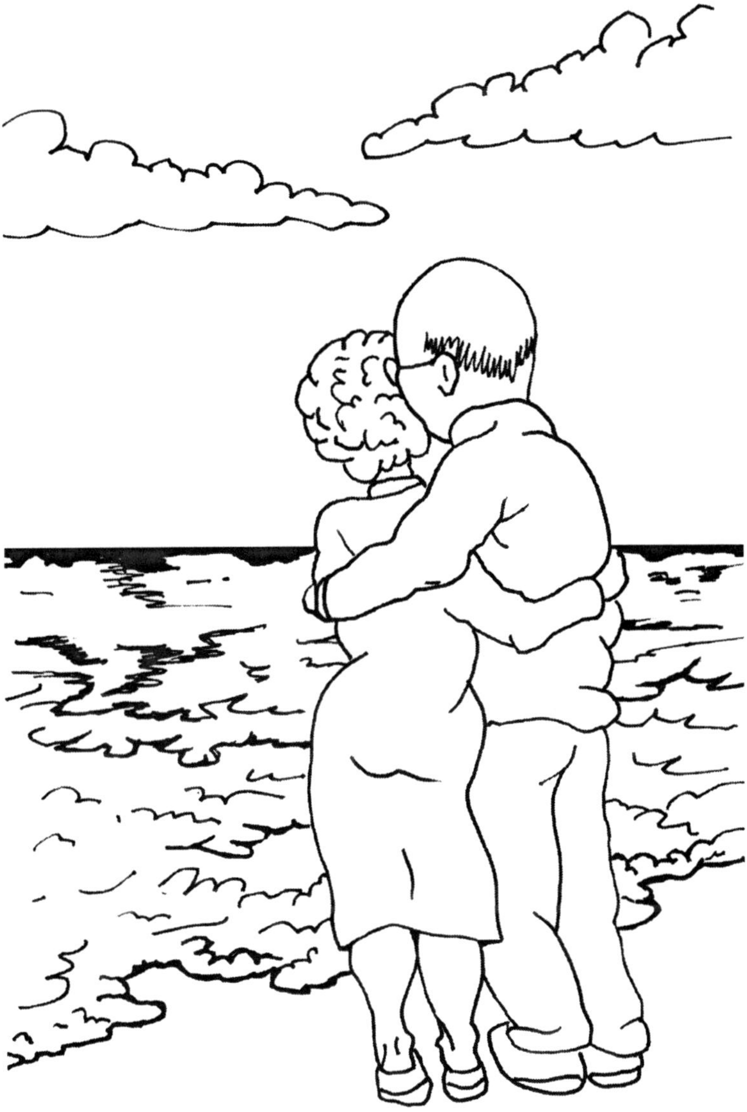

Alas, Poor Torek

Artifex Longus

Torek's a graffiti artist.
Critics rave that he's the smartest,
Baddest of the urban aces
Who enhance our public spaces.

Subway cars and buildings bleed
Words and symbols none can read,
Save each fellow vandal, cast
As today's iconoclast,

Marking turf like alpha dogs,
Cheering every serf who slogs
Past their sprayed-on masterworks.
Little people—tellers, clerks—
Should be grateful for the color
Artists bring to lives much duller.
Shame on any storefront boor,
Scraping art that should endure.

Torek rules since he's been crowned
Art world king—intense, profound.
Highbrows brand as "clearly orphic"
Glyphs, perversely polymorphic:

Prophecies by Delphic priest,
Warnings at Belshazzar's Feast,
Mockings of the wealthy pigs—
Wall Street types with penthouse digs,
Who will bleed their salaries,
Buying him in galleries.

Torek's bored with all the glory
Canvas brings him. Sixteenth-story
Ledges proved much more exciting.
He must make a statement—biting,
Daring, larger by degrees,
Big as Christo's wrapping sprees.

Torek's gutsy new production
Happens where immense construction
On a dam is nearly finished.
Stealth and cunning undiminished,
He's rappelled with sacks of paint,
Armed to leave, without restraint,
On the face of Culver Dam:
"Behold ye mighty! Torek am!"

He pulls a can out of his sack,
Prepared to start. But then a crack!
A snap! Now Torek, paint and all,
Is earthward bound. Oh no! His fall
Gains speed as Torek hurls toward
A bed of concrete, freshly poured.
He sinks at least one hundred feet.
The surface heals so clean and neat
That no one ever learns his fate.
The art world mourns. So young, so great.
A cryptic loss to be lamented,
Yet to the ages he's cemented.

Hale Mary

Mary was a flight attendant
When her youth was still ascendant:
Pert, alert, and flirty too.
Now she's well past thirty-two—

Close to fifty I would guess.
Yet the woman still can dress
Breezily in summer eyelet.
When she's standing with her pilot

Husband, what a striking pair!
Kids in college? That's not fair!
Skin of peach and hair of honey,
Disposition always sunny,

Tiny-waisted, tasteful Mary
Went to work as secretary
For a middle manager.
She addressed her boss as "Sir,"

Brought him coffee fixed just so,
Made him feel a CEO.
She's that way with all the guys:
Fixes collars, straightens ties.

Feeling Mary touch his collar,
Blushing, each feels bigger, taller.
You would guess the women hate her
As they watch her fawn and cater

To the men who love her touch.
Yet they like her rather much.
Mary's charmed them, truth to tell—
Save the head of personnel.

Even she of jaundiced eye
Cried when she saw Mary cry.
"Certainly," she had to answer
When she learned that Mary's cancer

Made her meekly ask for one day
Off each week, say every Monday?
Who could question that request?
Therapy might save her breast.

All the staff felt bad for Mary,
Lauding her extraordinary
Courage and her quiet strength.
Could she beat the thing at length?

Several months of treatment passed
When Ms. Personnel, aghast,
Saw a strong and chipper Mary
On a Monday at a very

Grand affair, a luncheon formed to
Aid a cause the firm had warmed to
Down at the convention center.
As she's sipping coffee, enter

Mary, supervising staff
On the caterer's behalf.
Mary Jones was double-dipping
With a second job at Lipping

Caterers! No toleration!
This was cause for termination!
Then the damnedest thing occurred,
Proving life is just absurd.

Overnight a corporate coup.
Knives were bared. Result: a new
CEO—one Franklin Perry
Who was very fond of Mary.

Deaf to Personnel's demands,
Franklin Staunton Perry stands
Firm defending Mary's honor,
Heaping lots of praise upon her.

Now she sits outside his door—
Placid, smiling, even more
Lovely, but a bit more distant,
As Executive Assistant.

Reader, do you think it odd
She should triumph, tempting God?
Pleasant, sweet, and so corrupt,
Mary wins, for she's one-upped

Personnel and all the Furies—
Even God's seraphic juries.
So we leave her, calmly sipping
Coffee, fixed just so by Lipping

At a catered lunch with Mister
Perry, who has since dismissed her
Nemesis in Personnel.
Who knew things could end so well?

One more thing, perhaps worth noting:
If a cad should stoop to voting
There among the female guests,
Mary wins for firmest breasts.

Mary used the extra bucks
From her extra job for tucks—
Firming assets. Hail the Cheater!
Even gravity can't beat her.

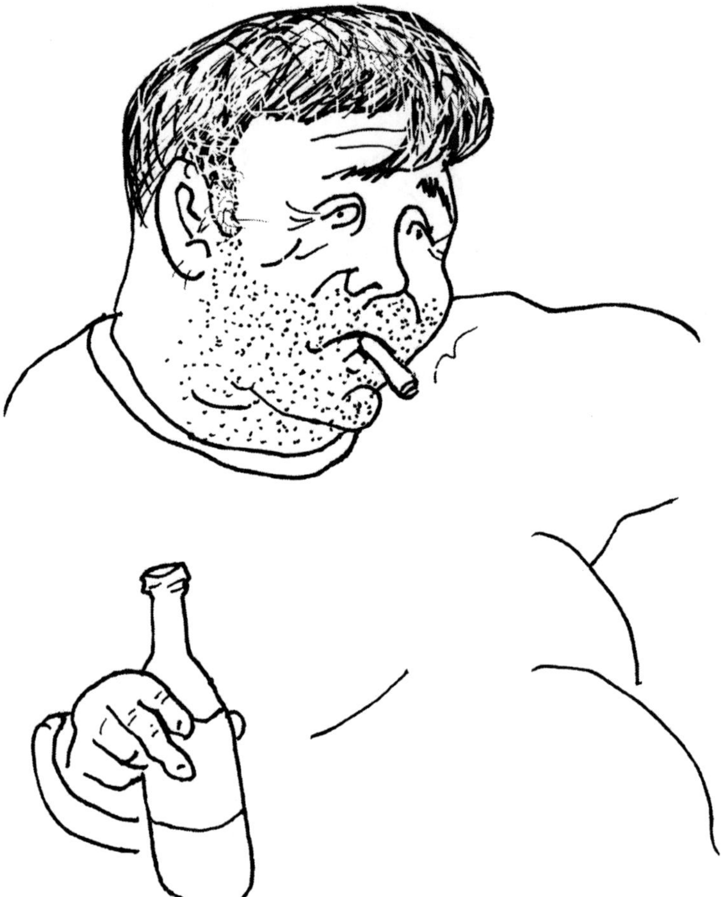

Garrison Goodbody

Garrison Goodbody isn't ambitious.
He watches his Razorbacks game on TV.
Smoking a cigarette, hearing the dishes
Clink in the sink as they're washed by Marie.
"Honey, that dinner was really delicious.
Another beer, baby, whenever you're free."
Thinking of glory days, Garrison wishes
Life could be all that it once used to be,
Back when he scrimmaged for St. Aloysius,
Back when his jersey still fit to a T.
Garrison curses the workplace as vicious.
Since his dismissal, he's been lost at sea.
Cigarettes low, now he eagerly fishes
Coins from the cushions. Hooray! He's found three.

Garrison's always had things pretty easy—
Tall and good looking and sporting a glow,
Scoring with women, from proper to sleazy,
Watching them melt at his sexy "hello."
Now his "hello" is less sexy than wheezy.
Maybe that's why they've begun to say "no."
Yet, with the guys he can still shoot the breeze. He
Rules in the sports bar where fans hear him crow
How, if he hadn't destroyed both his knees, he
Certainly, easily could have gone pro.
Salesman instead, but he starred in those cheesy
Auto commercials: "Say 'hi' and buy low!
Just off Route 7! I'm holding your keys!" he
Shouted to viewers as star of the show.

Single now, Garrison did have a prior
Marriage to Darlington's then beauty queen.
Didn't last long. Hell, they both were on fire—
Burning with lust, and yet so young and green.
One inconvenience: he did quickly sire
Gordon, who now—is he really sixteen?
Such is the baggage that comes from desire.
She wanted kids. Well, you know the routine.
Post-divorce, shouting and angry, she'd ply her
Tears at the dealership, making a scene.
He missed some payments so *she* pierced a tire
On his Corvette. Man, was that a machine!
Had the judge garnish his wages. The liar
Won even more "for the kid." God, she's mean.

Doorbell rings. Who could it be at this hour?
Drying her hands, Marie opens the door.
Thunder and lightning as rain torrents shower
Gordon, tattooed. And he's pierced to the core.
Skinny and pale, and as frail as a flower,
Gordon's gone goth. As he drips on the floor,
Garrison, speechless, just stares with a glower
At his mascara. He looks like a whore!
Hair dyed jet-black in a now sagging tower—
This is the son he's been paying out for?
"Come on in, kid. Don't just stand there and cower,"
(Said in a rather unwelcoming roar).
"Can the beer, honey. Make mine whiskey sour.
Gordon and I have some things to explore."

Gordon's been living with friends for a while.
Dropped out of school, which he kind of regrets.
Just a few weeks, but already a trial.
"Didn't work out, Dad," he says as he sweats.
"Wondered if I could move in." Soon a smile
Tugs at his mouth as he fidgets and frets.
Silence. Then Garrison, sighing, says, "I'll
Check with Marie. But don't make any bets.
Carrying *me*'s bad enough. Not her style
To act like it is, but we're drowning in debts.
Morning, I'll go through my contacts and dial
Around to see who might have jobs for us. Let's
Clean ourselves up and get off our shit pile.
Son, could I bum one of your cigarettes?"

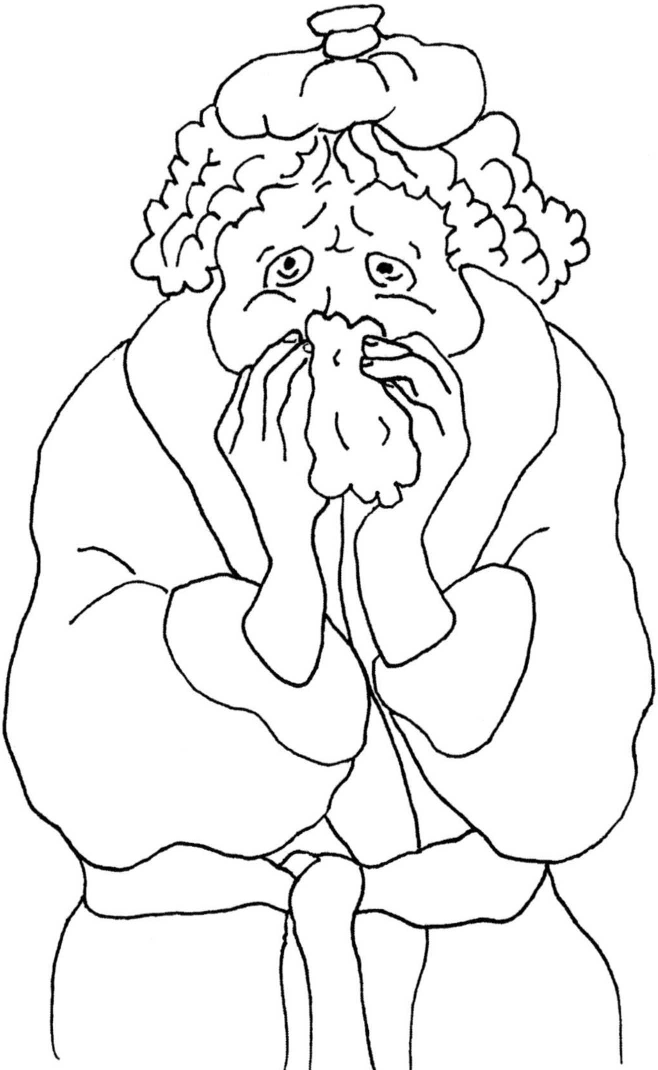

Melody McMallidy

Melody McMallidy has aches from top to bottom:
Headaches, ulcers, leg cramps, corns. . .
You name 'em and she's got 'em—
From summer ills to winter chills
To allergies in autumn.

She has each illness catalogued
From nose to nervous system.
And you don't even have to ask.
She's more than glad to list 'em,
Repeating those she's proudest of
In case you might have missed 'em.

She's very kind. When neighbors ail,
In minutes she is off
With soup to ask them how they feel;
But very soon, she'll scoff,
"You think that's bad? I got it worse.
Just listen to this cough!"

Poor Melody McMallidy. Today she has a fever.
I hear her telling neighbors of the latest pain to grieve her.
And all the neighbors pity her.
And none of them believe her.

The Devil and Crazy Eddie

You've seen Crazy Eddie, unsteady on crutches.
He's cursed with afflictions, quite nearly as much as
Old Job could endure; and he's sure he's the victim
Of Satan himself, who has pricked him and kicked him.
But God rules it all, so perhaps He has sicced him
On Eddie to test him. Who'll wrest him from sin?
If Eddie gives in, then the Devil will win.

His trials on earth start at birth when his mother
Delivers a babe hooked on one or the other
Narcotic she smoked or else poked in her arm.
She swore that she never intended to harm
The Littlest Junkie. "My monkey," she called him,
And walled him away till the city installed him
In halls with the others deformed and deprived.
Then came the bright day when a couple arrived
To offer him kindness and cure him with love.
He answered each hug with a slug or a shove.

It never got better. Their chronic bed wetter
Could not have a buddy that he wouldn't bloody
Before very long, and no talks in the study
With Dad seemed to matter. Just chatter
To ears filled with fears from the years
When his birth mom would batter
Him silly until he was taken away.
And then came the day when he started to steal—
First money, then pills from the cabinet to deal
On the street, where he'd meet all the users,
Abusers, and various losers until he was caught.
Then he fought his accusers in court
Many times till his parents, in short,
Just surrendered. They tendered a forced separation,
With subsidized rent in a decent location.

By now he was twenty with plenty of time
To get into jams, never thinking to climb
From out of the sewer or ever mature.
So then, with resources grown scanter and fewer,
He teamed with a lawyer he'd seen on TV
Who asked for no fee. Well, except for a share
Of the winnings. The pair of them sued
Eddie's folks with the hoax of a case, and they won!
So the fun had begun. And before they were done,
They would then sue the city
In case after case, where by grace of the pity
Of juries, his worries with money would pass
Until all was but dust—up his nostrils, alas.

Now Eddie, quite grayed and decayed, is seen splayed
In a frayed, dirty blanket on Axelrod Street.
At his feet is a sign with the words, "HELP ME EAT."
And beside him, his crutches. It touches the heart
Of the people who pass and are willing to part
With some change for the can of this strange, broken man.

But what of the sparring twixt Satan and God
For Eddie's sweet soul (on the whole, pretty flawed)?
Has God truly lost him or tossed him away
And ousted our Faust whom the devil made prey?
Not so. For though Eddie was heady and hateful,
Dishonest, dissembling, unyielding, ungrateful,
At last he's found love, and through love, a beginning.
He's winning the war against Satan and sinning.

He has a new life with a common-law wife
They call Crazy Sadie. He calls her his lady—
His Gretchen, a wretch in some tattered old rags,
Who pushes her bags in a cart as she drags

Some hits from a cigarette tossed on the street.
His day's work complete, Eddie's now on his feet,
So he gathers his rather sad work tools, and counts
The amounts in his cup. Then it's up to the ridge
And his shipping crate home nestled under a bridge
Where she's waiting for him in the dim evening light.
She's a beautiful sight though she's missing her teeth,
Because Eddie sees only the soul underneath,
Just as shining and lovely and perfect in form
As Our Lady of Lourdes. Loving Eddie will warm
Her with kisses and hugs underneath an old spread
As he quiets the voices she hears in her head.

Ordelia O'Fonely

What's wrong with Ordelia?
She finds life so tough.
She's pretty, but somehow
Not pretty enough.

She has a nice figure.
But you can see better
On magazine covers.
Those models upset her.

They carry themselves
With the bearing of queens.
If only she also
Had gotten those genes.

She worships celebrities,
Loving their glitter.
Those red-carpet gowns!
If only they'd fit her!

The beautiful rule
And the rest of us serve them.
They're so far above us,
We scarcely deserve them.

She hardly can look
At herself in a mirror.
If only her skin were
A little bit clearer.

If only her height
Were a little bit taller.
Oh why did such ugliness
Have to befall her?

Now flash to the future.
She's reached middle age.
She thumbs through an album
And stops at a page:

Her face in a photo,
So lovely back then.
If only she looked half
That lovely again.

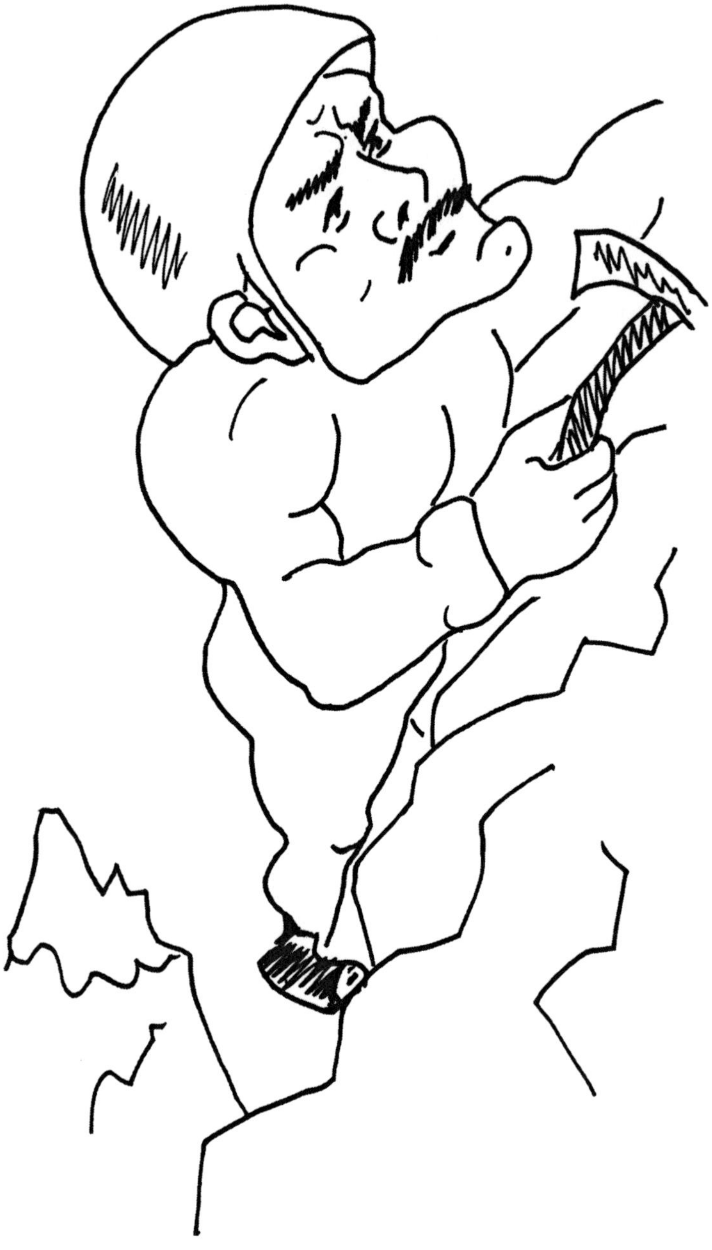

Rod Rockwell, Mountain Tamer

One can assume it began in the womb
Where he kicked at his twin when there wasn't much room
For them both any longer; and he, being stronger,
Was first down the chute, the cute little brute.

His force would continue. And not just by sinew.
When you have to win, you don't stop with your twin. You
Develop your brain to maintain your domain.
The playground and classroom were venues to gain
Prominence, dominance: Long did he reign.

But being a leader just wasn't enough.
Our hero must show he is forged from the stuff
That made the conquistadors so tough and rough.

It was all about him. He was grimly committed
To proving himself to the world; so he pitted
His might against Nature, and always acquitted
Himself with assurance, endurance, and grit.
You had to admit he was fit, if a bit . . .

Well, on with his story, his glory, his quest.
The man mounted mountains, as onward he pressed.
"Why stop at the top? Why rest at the crest,
With still higher peaks that will test all your best?
And blizzards be damned!" Should his Sherpas protest,

He would go it alone. He was hewn out of stone.
If those with him failed, then he scaled on his own,
Deserting the wounded, the weakened, the frail
To find their way back down the track or the trail.
He couldn't be bothered to ease their travail.

If Rod wasn't loved, he just shoved that aside.
He couldn't care less. Weaker beings might chide.
Superior spirits just take it in stride.

No wife and no chums. But now comes an event
To test him beyond any rocky ascent.
Awaiting a train in the subway's dim hollows,
A bag lady falls to the rails and he follows.
Not blinking or thinking, he tosses her back.
The train leaves him bloodied and dead on the track.

At last, for the least, in a moment he's bought
Her life with his own without giving it thought,
And found in that act all the glory he sought.

One can divine he is cutting in line,
Clutching a form for St. Peter to sign,
Stressing and pressing to hurry the queue.
Death is so short and there's so much to do:
Cumulous clouds he is itching to climb.
"Let me through, folks. Don't those peaks look sublime?
You all died much older, but I'm in my prime."

Eternity offers us too little time.

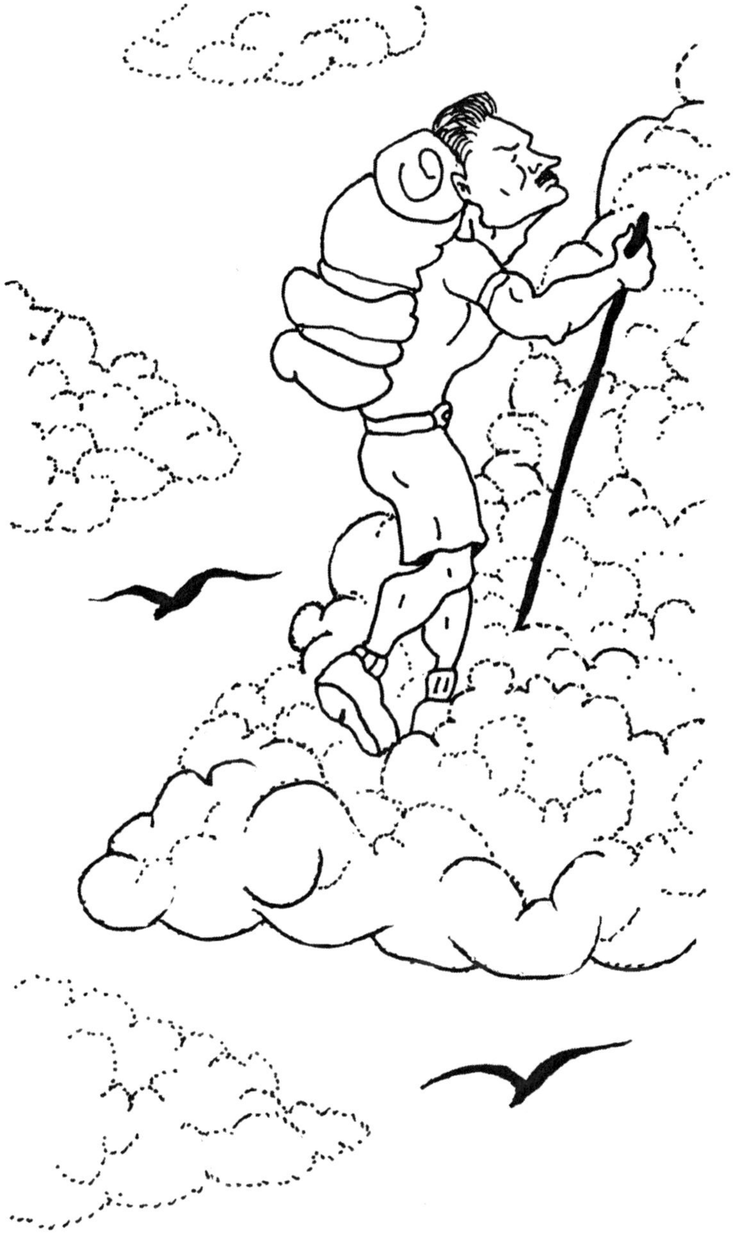

Closing Time

Poor Arnold the greeter's asleep in his chair.
We leave Mrs. Young as she's dyeing her hair.
Miss Quigley is vacantly stroking a cat.
Dolores del Sangre's alone in her flat.
It's probably best that we call it a day.
But let's not forget as we wander away
That some of the cages we found occupied
Are now standing empty, like those at their side.
So please turn the page for a word from your guide.

ZOO
CLOSED

Dear Reader

Dear Reader, now our stroll has reached its end.
There's always more to see another day.
A safe drive home I wish you, gentle friend,
And leave you with a thought to guide your way.

A Sonnet on It

A shock to wake and find that you exist.
It's such a scary thing to be alive:
To clutch the wheel of self and have to drive
With scant instruction through a heavy mist
On roads unmarked, with sudden drop and twist.
While many drivers panic, some will thrive.
Not caring if or how they may arrive,
But thrilling to the challenge, they persist.

However we respond, we're still the bearers
Of consequence from choices we have made.
Of all we face or flee, of all our errors,
By our own fears are we the most betrayed.
God placed us in a world so full of terrors,
And all that's asked is we not be afraid.

CPSIA information can be obtained at www.ICGtesting.com
Printed in the USA
LVOW052147240213

321442LV00002B/26/P